Gone with the winds

This is actually my second book inspired by farts. The first was the one hundred and twenty-eight page scholastic version of "Heidi" that Mrs. Barnum made me write out longhand after an incident in fourth grade.

We were in the middle of our two o'clock English class. Mrs. Barnum was at the blackboard busily diagramming a compound sentence when the silence was fractured by a series of loud noises. It was as if someone was desperately trying to start a chain saw. Underwater.

In Mrs. Barnum's defense, let me say that the school's hot lunch program presented us with a particularly tough choice that afternoon. Meatloaf, usually more gristle than meat or the sloppy joes, which often had unpredictable gastronomic side effects.

The first three rows realized instantly Mrs. Barnum had opted for the sloppy joes.

With several of my classmates already overcome by fumes, I did the only thing I could. I leaped from my seat, grabbed the window pole which was a long stick with a hook on the end and used it to fling open one window, then another and another.

As I reached the fourth window, Mrs. Barnum reached my right ear. The loud laughter of my classmates quickly subsided as I was lifted over several desks by the ear and dragged to the principal's office.

My punishment was to write out the first five chapters of "Heidi". When I innocently questioned her knowledge of the current copyright statutes the assignment was expanded from cover to cover.

Eventually, the slack in my right ear tightened somewhat leaving it only ten inches longer than my left. Recently, I've taken to spray painting it black and laying it over the top of my head to cover my bald spot. So you see, everything works out in the end.

Enjoy the book,
Mike Fornwald

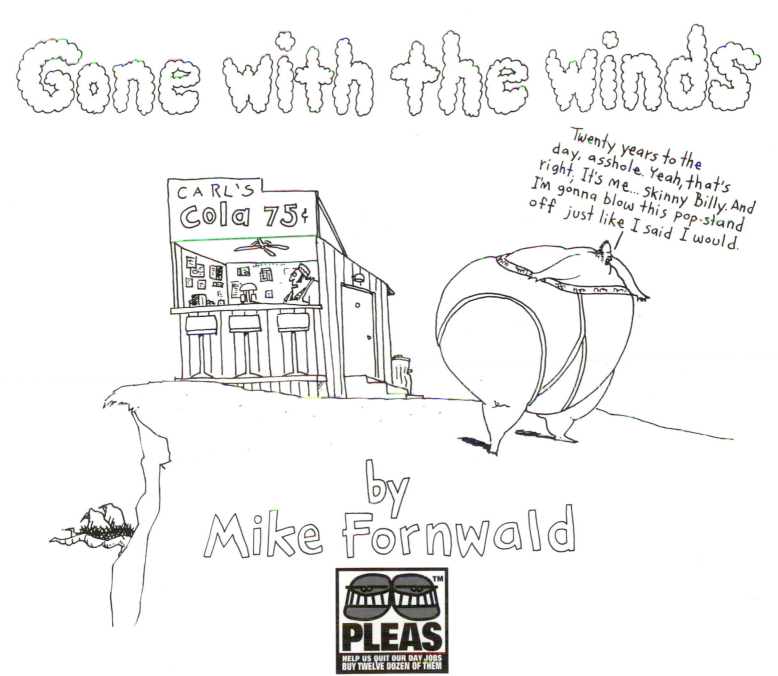

Basically, we're just a bunch of average schmucks wanting a second chance at doing something else for a living.

I don't know one person alive who didn't object to having this fart book dedicated to them. I then dedicate this book to my mother, Kathleen O'Brien, who is not here to defend herself.

Of the 91 drawings in this collection, 91 of them did not appear in <u>The New Yorker.</u>

Turd Edition

Library of Congress Catalog Card Number: 94-92440

ISBN: 0-9643845-0-7

Published by Pleas Ltd, P.O. Box 17315, Milwaukee, Wisconsin 53217-0315

For a teeny weeny catalog of paraphernalia... send a stamped, self addressed envelope to the publisher at the address above.

Printed in the United States of America.

Fornwald

The grain exchange

Fornwald

Force field

A fart coming on

How Nick really is at night

Fornwald

One of life's stupid mysteries

Fornwald

Fornwald

Fornwald

Ass transit

Fornwald

Fornwald

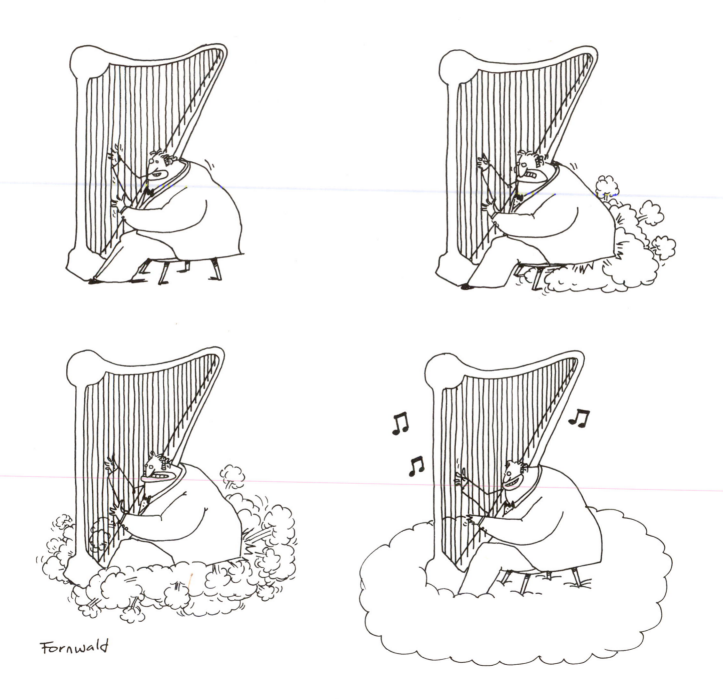

Fornwald

Reporting from the news 4 copter, the storm that brought with it high winds, quickly intensified, causing what we're calling from our position, a devastating mud slide...

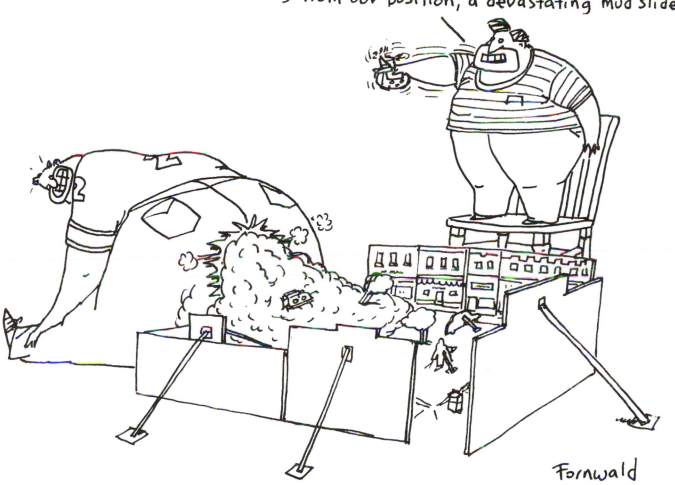

Fornwald

Contrails

Fornwald

30

Millie Johnson's version of
the NBC peacock

Fornwald

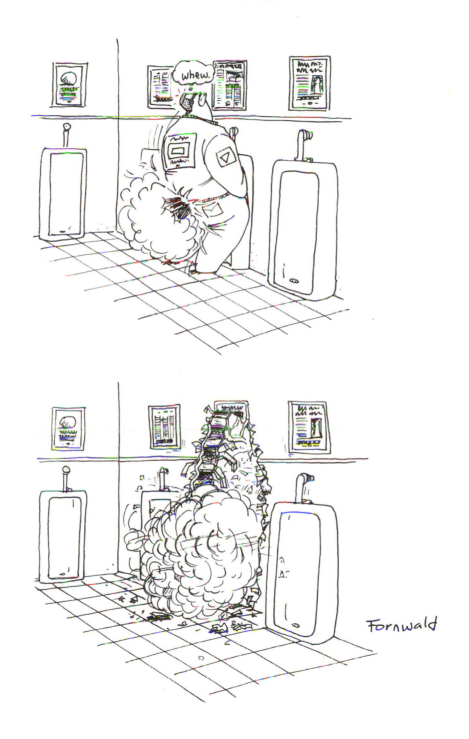

My achy breaky fart

Just one of the many disadvantages
of living your life ass-backwards

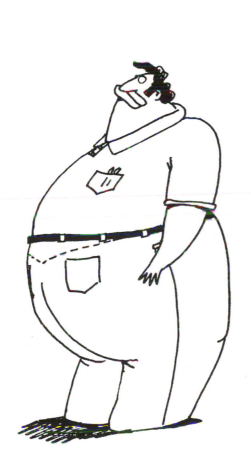

Fornwald

kissing Grim Ripper Ass

How it really happened

Watch uncle dick pull an animal out his ass.

What's that? I hear him barking.

His father was a chili-burrito.

And the mother was part show poodle and part rectum.

Fornwald

Sooner or later every fart finds out for itself

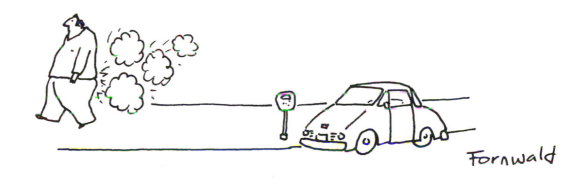

Fornwald

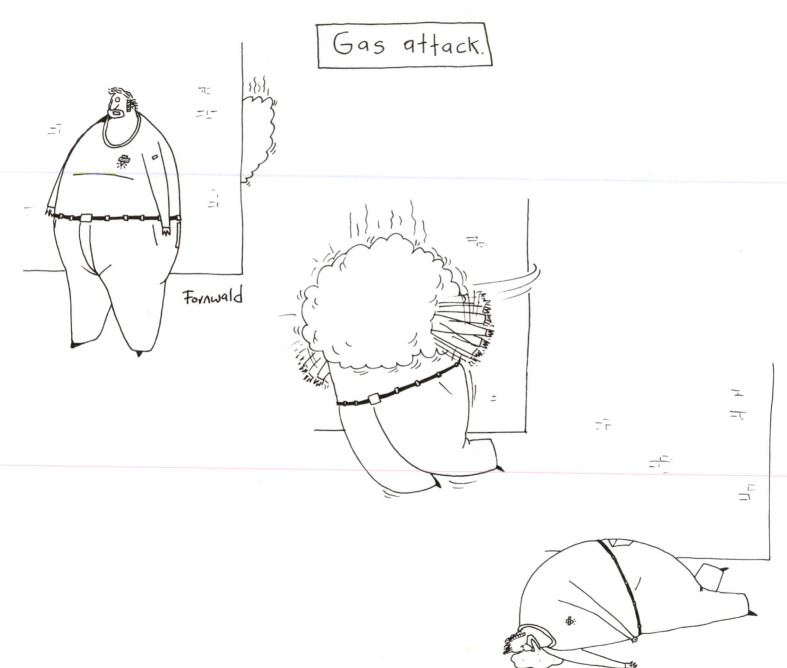

Gas attack.

Fornwald

Fornwald

Fornwald

49

A passing fancy

Fornwald

The relief pitcher's nightmare: Liquid farts

Fornwald

Cooking with gas

The Direct Method

The Indirect Method

Fornwald

53

The wind section

Fornwald

Fornwald

Cocooning in the 90's

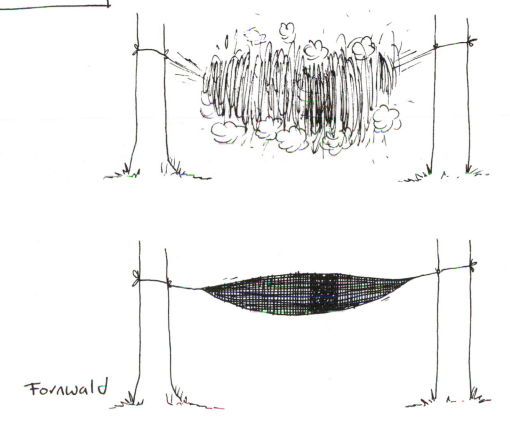

Fornwald

Fornwald

The explosion shot

Now that the gallery has cleared it's easy to see why his playing partners quit on him... but, as golf shots go, he does have a soft shot out of the bunkers.

All I can say is whew.

18

AMATEUR 94

Fornwald

Fornwald

63

Fornwald

A baker's dozen

Fornwald

Silent Partners

Fornwald

Behind enemy lines

Suddenly, the room emptied in seconds as Doreen's boyfriend (former) of two days mistakenly asked her dad, sporting his favorite kidney bean shirt to, "Pass the Potatoes."

Fornwald

Unrecorded history: September 12, 1979, Harry Houdini lives up to his promise and escapes from the grave

Fornwald

The surefire way to get the remote

(A) Unload liberal amounts of gas on victim's body.

(B) Ask unpolitely for remote.

(C) Grasp remote firmly while calling the victim a fool.

(D) Let the fireworks begin.

Fornwald

Early flying carpet

Fornwald

Laying the big turd at the office

Fornwald

Fornwald

The blind leading the blind

Fornwald

Elimination race

Fornwald

83

Furniture stress test laboratory

Fornwald

The exit interview gone bad

Fornwald

Smelling Salts

Fornwald

It was the best of times.

Fornwald

It was the worst of times.

Fornwald

The 7 habits of highly flatulent people

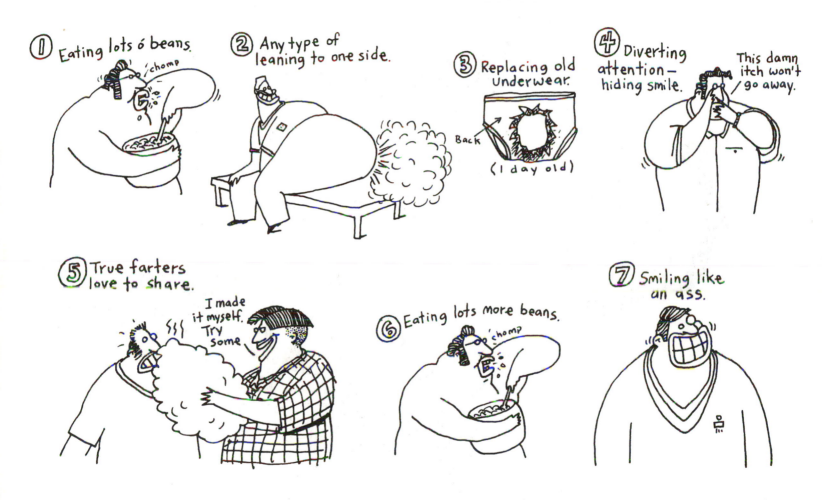

Fornwald

The organic gas chamber

Notice the tension mounting as the executioner finishes off the last of 120 bowls of beans and cabbage.

Fornwald